W9-AUQ-072

Thinking Critically: Online Privacy

Christine Wilcox

San Diego, CA

© 2015 ReferencePoint Press, Inc.
Printed in the United States

For more information, contact:
ReferencePoint Press, Inc.
PO Box 27779
San Diego, CA 92198
www.ReferencePointPress.com

Picture Credits:
Thinkstock Images: 9
Maury Aaseng: 15, 22, 29, 36, 41, 48, 56, 61

LIBRARY OF CONGRESS CATALOGING-IN-PUBLICATION DATA

Wilcox, Christine.
  Thinking critically: Online privacy / by Christine Wilcox.
    pages cm. — (Thinking critically)
  Includes bibliographical references and index.
  ISBN-13: 978-1-60152-734-9 (hardback)
  ISBN-10: 1-60152-734-9 (hardback)
  1. Privacy, Right of—Juvenile literature. 2. Internet users—Juvenile literature. 3. Electronic surveillance—Juvenile literature. I. Title.
  JC596.W56 2015
  323.44'802854678—dc23
                                                            2014006449

Contents

Foreword

"Literacy is the most basic currency of the knowledge economy we're living in today." Barack Obama (at the time a senator from Illinois) spoke these words during a 2005 speech before the American Library Association. One question raised by this statement is: What does it mean to be a literate person in the twenty-first century?

E.D. Hirsch Jr., author of *Cultural Literacy: What Every American Needs to Know*, answers the question this way: "To be culturally literate is to possess the basic information needed to thrive in the modern world. The breadth of the information is great, extending over the major domains of human activity from sports to science."

But literacy in the twenty-first century goes beyond the accumulation of knowledge gained through study and experience and expanded over time. Now more than ever literacy requires the ability to sift through and evaluate vast amounts of information and, as the authors of the Common Core State Standards state, to "demonstrate the cogent reasoning and use of evidence that is essential to both private deliberation and responsible citizenship in a democratic republic."

The Thinking Critically series challenges students to become discerning readers, to think independently, and to engage and develop their skills as critical thinkers. Through a narrative-driven, pro/con format, the series introduces students to the complex issues that dominate public discourse—topics such as gun control and violence, social networking, and medical marijuana. All chapters revolve around a single, pointed question such as Can Stronger Gun Control Measures Prevent Mass Shootings?, or Does Social Networking Benefit Society?, or Should Medical Marijuana Be Legalized? This inquiry-based approach introduces student researchers to core issues and concerns on a given topic. Each chapter includes one part that argues the affirmative and one part that argues the negative—all written by a single author. With the single-author format the predominant arguments for and against an issue can be synthesized into clear, accessible discussions supported by details and evidence including relevant facts, direct quotes, current examples, and statistical illustrations. All volumes include focus questions to guide students as they read each pro/con discussion, a list of key facts, and an annotated list of related organizations and websites for conducting further research.

The authors of the Common Core State Standards have set out the particular qualities that a literate person in the twenty-first century must have. These include the ability to think independently, establish a base of knowledge across a wide range of subjects, engage in open-minded but discerning reading and listening, know how to use and evaluate evidence, and appreciate and understand diverse perspectives. The new Thinking Critically series supports these goals by providing a solid introduction to the study of pro/con issues.

Online Privacy

In April 2012 an information technology (IT) contractor for the National Security Agency (NSA) named Edward Snowden began to download thousands of documents about the US government's secret mass surveillance programs. Snowden had deliberately taken the contracting job with the NSA to gather information that showed how the government regularly violated citizens' privacy. In June 2013 the global news organization the *Guardian* broke the first of many stories about the content of those documents, revealing to the world that the US government routinely monitored Internet traffic and collected and stored massive amounts of data—often from American citizens. When asked why he stole and leaked the documents, Snowden explained, "It was seeing a continuing litany of lies from senior officials to Congress—and therefore the American people—and the realization that Congress . . . wholly supported the lies."[1]

The documents leaked by Snowden, who relocated to Russia to avoid prosecution in the United States, sparked a national debate about online privacy. The debate began with concerns about government monitoring of people's online activities but has since expanded to include all aspects of online privacy. During this period of reflection and debate, people have learned that what they do online is being monitored by big corporations, which compile detailed profiles on the online habits of everyone who surfs the web. Electronic health records, which are mandated by the American Recovery and Reinvestment Act of 2009, have also come under criticism as people worry that their health information is vulnerable to hackers or government surveillance. Responding to these concerns, privacy advocates have called for more

6

regulation, and states have started passing laws to protect online privacy. Some people have disabled tracking features on their web browsers and taken other precautions. Others wonder if online privacy is even possible.

What Is Data Mining?

One term that comes up in the debate again and again is *data mining*. Data mining is defined by the *Merriam-Webster* online dictionary as "the practice of searching through large amounts of computerized data to find useful patterns or trends."[2] Companies have been collecting and mining data for decades, using the technique to analyze and predict everything from their own future earnings to the buying habits of their customers. But with today's powerful computers and online tracking tools, businesses now have the ability to learn much more about individuals, including their present—and future—interests, habits, financial worth, and even health status.

Every time Internet users make a purchase, fill out a form, play a game, or enable GPS on a mobile device, companies can glean valuable information about those users' likes, dislikes, and habits. Some companies use this data to help sell their products, but others are in the business of creating and selling detailed consumer profiles. These companies are called data brokerage firms, and they have been known to collect up to fifteen hundred pieces of data about each individual, such as how much time they spend on various websites, who and what they "like" on Facebook, and what they say in public posts to social media sites. From this information the firms can predict the likelihood that an individual will purchase a particular product and then sell his or her profile to a company that sells that product.

> "It was seeing a continuing litany of lies from senior officials to Congress—and therefore the American people—and the realization that Congress. . . wholly supported the lies."[1]
>
> —Former NSA analyst Edward Snowden, on why he leaked thousands of top secret NSA documents to the press.

Behavioral Tracking and Targeted Advertising

Companies collect data on Internet users through a technique called behavioral tracking. When a user visits a website, the site's advertising partners install small text files known as cookies on the user's computer. Cookies let them know what people are doing online, such as what websites they visit and what links they have clicked. "This lets advertisers build a profile of you in the hope you'll be more susceptible to marketing messages," technology expert Dennis Kügler explains. "Cookies have therefore become essential to the online ad industry. Not only do they allow advertisers to target ads to your individual tastes, they also track whether or not an advertisement is effective."[3]

Cookies also determine what type of ad to display when a user navigates to another partner site. This is called targeted advertising, and it is far more effective than traditional advertising methods. Traditional advertising usually relies on the context of an ad, rather than the behavior of a consumer. For instance, television commercials assume things about viewers based on the programs they watch. Cartoons are filled with ads for children's toys, and daytime shows often feature products useful to stay-at-home parents. Targeted advertising is far more specific. Instead of showing ads for cat food on a website featuring cute cats, targeted advertising will instead show ads for the washing machine a specific user was researching an hour earlier.

Targeted advertising is the current business model of most companies that advertise on the Internet. The revenue generated from targeted advertising also pays for most of the free content the web has to offer. Most of the controversy that surrounds targeted advertising, and the behavioral tracking and data mining that power it, has to do with whether or not the free content available on the web is worth the sacrifices to personal privacy caused by data mining and behavioral tracking.

Online Privacy and National Security

Before Snowden's revelations, most people assumed that their privacy was protected from government intrusion by the Fourth Amendment, which prevents unreasonable search and seizure. However, after the

8

Companies gather valuable information about the likes, dislikes, and habits of Internet users who make online purchases, fill out online forms, play online games, and even enable GPS on their mobile devices. Some companies use this data to help sell their products, but others are in the business of creating and selling detailed consumer profiles.

September 11, 2001, terrorist attacks, Congress passed the Patriot Act, which limited Fourth Amendment protections and greatly expanded the right of the government to gather intelligence in its fight against terrorism. A provision of the Patriot Act also allows the government to demand from Internet companies everything from e-mail to browsing history, which companies like Facebook and Google keep on file for several years. The Patriot Act also prohibits those companies from letting their customers—or anyone else—know that they have released data to the government.

After leaked documents revealed that the NSA had been collecting data from large Internet companies in bulk, many small Internet companies that specialize in online privacy decided to shut down rather than be put in a position in which they had to turn over data to the government. Silent Circle, an Internet communication company that promises complete confidentiality to its customers, shut down its e-mail service in 2013. Silent Circle CEO Mike Janke told the *Washington Post*, "There are some very high profile, highly targeted groups of people [among the firm's customers]. We felt we were going to be targeted, without a doubt."[4]

Privacy and Electronic Health Records

In the health-care industry, information enjoys much stronger online protections than consumer data. The Health Insurance Portability and Accountability Act (HIPAA) guarantees patients the right to privacy and specifies security standards for health information that must be maintained to keep data private. HIPAA also applies to electronic health records, or EHRs. EHRs are becoming more and more common among health-care providers. This is partly because the American Recovery and Reinvestment Act of 2009 gave doctors and hospitals financial incentives to transition from paper-based records to EHRs and mandated that they do so by 2015. The incentives appear to have worked: By April 2013, 50 percent of doctors and 80 percent of hospitals had made the transition to EHRs, up from 17 percent of doctors and 9 percent of hospitals in 2008.

Many privacy advocates are concerned that these EHRs have been set up too quickly, without proper attention to training and security, and that HIPAA privacy standards cannot be properly maintained. EHRs—especially those used by hospitals—can give thousands of people online access to health data. These include low-level health-care workers, government workers, and even private sector entities like Microsoft's HealthVault—one of the many patient portals that allow patients to view and easily interact with their own health records. While major privacy breaches of EHRs are rare, they have the potential to be much more damaging than breaches to consumer data because health information is so sensitive.

Does the Law Protect Online Privacy?

As the Internet has expanded to affect nearly every aspect of public and private life, privacy advocates have pushed lawmakers to fix outdated laws, as well as to address the many new privacy issues facing the nation today. So far only state governments have passed meaningful online privacy reform. One reason the federal government has not been able to update privacy laws is because of lobbying efforts by online businesses. More federal regulation would obstruct advertising and suppress online business, they argue, which would not only harm the economy but would reduce the amount of information and services that are available for free on the Internet.

Do Not Track legislation has become the center of the debate. Advocates like Senator Al Franken from Minnesota have argued, "People have a right to privacy. It's a fundamental right, and they have a right to know what's being taken and stored and how it's being used."[5] Despite this argument, attempts to pass federal Do Not Track legislation have stalled.

> "People have a right to privacy. It's a fundamental right, and they have a right to know what's being taken and stored and how it's being used."[5]
>
> —Al Franken, senator from Minnesota.

So have attempts within the online industry to come up with universal best practices for consumer privacy and online tracking. According to Jaron Lanier, author of *You Are Not a Gadget*, "The problem with privacy regulations is that they are unlikely to be followed. Big data statistics become an addiction, and privacy regulations are like drug or alcohol prohibitions."[6] In other words, the temptation for those in power to keep things as they are may be too great, because the current online business climate is extremely profitable.

In the end American citizens may have to vote with their wallets if they want to pressure companies to adopt privacy standards. Until then, the debate continues.

Chapter One

Do the Benefits of Commercial Data Mining Outweigh the Risks to Privacy?

Commercial Data Mining Benefits the Individual and Society

- Data mining helps companies reach consumers.
- Data mining powers targeted advertising, which pays for free content on the web.
- Data mining powers services that help society.

The Debate at a Glance

Commercial Data Mining Infringes on Consumers' Privacy

- The information collected in data mining is far more revealing than most people realize.
- People's online activities are mined and monitored, not just the information they share.
- There is no way to opt out of data collection and data mining.

Commercial Data Mining Benefits the Individual and Society

"We need the online data industry in order to keep the web free. . . . It's the reason you don't pay a subscription fee for Google, Facebook or YouTube."

—Sam Barnett is the founder and CEO of the advertising company Struq.

Sam Barnett, "Privacy, Cookies and Free Web Content: Where Do We Go from Here?," *Guardian* (London), June 28, 2013. www.theguardian.com.

Consider these questions as you read:

1. How persuasive is the argument that the benefits of data mining outweigh the costs to privacy? Explain your answer.
2. One argument made here is that going outside is similar to going online in terms of sacrificing privacy. Do you think this is a good analogy? Why or why not?
3. Have you ever traded information about yourself for a product or service online, such as allowing a computer game to access your Facebook account so that you could play for free? Did the trade seem fair? Explain your answer.

Editor's note: The discussion that follows presents common arguments made in support of this perspective, reinforced by facts, quotes, and examples taken from various sources.

Data mining—the powerful technique that drives targeted advertising on the Internet—has created huge efficiencies for business. By analyzing the data left behind every time people go online, companies can compile detailed profiles that correctly predict who will buy a particular product. Many privacy advocates feel that this practice is intrusive, but the benefits of data mining—to the individual and to society—far outweigh any concerns about privacy.

Identifying Consumer Likes and Dislikes

One way that data mining benefits the individual is that it makes targeted advertising possible. Targeted advertising determines the interests of individual consumers and then shows them advertisements tailored to their interests. Most people are familiar with a common form of targeted advertising: behavioral targeting. When behavioral targeting is done over an ad network, users see ads based on their previous behavior online, such as visiting other websites that use the ad network. Behavioral targeting has proved to be far more effective than other online advertising techniques, such as matching an ad to a site's content (contextual advertising) or forcing a user to view an advertisement before delivering content (interstitial advertising).

> "Those personalized messages—'If you liked this book/movie/song then you might like these'—drive huge revenue."[7]
>
> —Data mining expert Andrew Cherwenka.

Data mining has made targeted advertising so effective that it can actually predict a consumer's likes and dislikes. This information can be used to create useful tools for consumers. For instance, companies like Netflix and Amazon use a form of data mining called predictive analytics to power their recommendation engines, which are extremely popular with consumers. According to data mining expert Andrew Cherwenka, "Those personalized messages—'If you liked this book/movie/song then you might like these'—drive huge revenue."[7] Some forms of predictive advertising are even more sophisticated. For instance, geo-targeting uses data from mobile devices to recognize a user's location. For example, marketing consultant Michael Leander writes,

McDonalds ran a campaign in Cairo [Egypt] where certain notifications or advertising messages were displayed directly within the CircleTie application [a local city guide mobile application] to CircleTie users searching for "fast food." This is a good example of an advanced advertising campaign where the display of the advertising message was based on both behavior, but also location of the user. As you may have guessed, the response rate was very high.[8]

Public Health Agencies Benefit from Google Data Mining

Public health officials have been able to predict the strength of flu outbreaks and better prepare for them thanks to Google's data mining capabilities. This Google Flu Trend graph estimates the intensity of flu outbreaks in the United States. The red line shows 2012–2013 data, and so on. Google Flu Trends is a Web service that uses Google search queries about flu symptoms to estimate flu activity in over twenty-five countries.

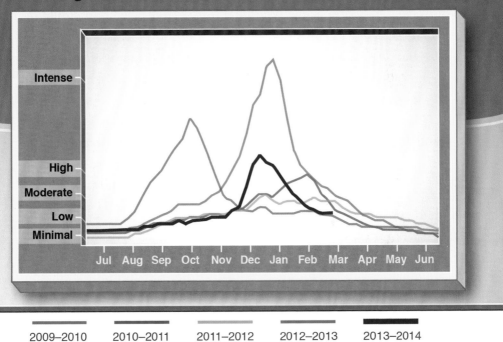

Google Flu Trends in the United States, 2009–2014

2009–2010   2010–2011   2011–2012   2012–2013   2013–2014

Source: Google.org Flu Trends, "Explore Flu Trends—United States," March 30, 2014. www.google.org.

Since 34 percent of people who go online do so mostly on mobile devices, advertising that takes advantage of location information is becoming more and more popular. This is true both for advertisers and consumers.

Privacy Is Not Violated

The data mining behind targeted advertising online has become so powerful that some people are concerned that companies may use their knowledge about consumers to defraud them or steal their identities. This simply is not happening. Consumer data mining merely analyzes data that is publicly available or legally obtained. This data is provided by consumers, who voluntarily share it when they visit a website.

Jim Harper, director of information policy studies at the Cato Institute, believes that consumers should view going online a lot like walking outside. "We lose control of personal information every time we go out[side]," he writes in the *New York Times*. "Your neighbors would see you as they hadn't before, make note of your movements, and probably talk about you some."[9] This, he explains, is what data mining essentially does—it makes inferences about you based on what you do, where you go, what you buy, and what you say online.

Direct mail advertisers, meaning those who send advertisements through the US Postal Service, buy the same information from data mining companies that online advertisers purchase. Like online advertisers, they target their mailings to people who are more likely to have an interest in their products, but no one ever complains that direct mail advertisers violate consumer privacy. "It's the monster-under-the-bed syndrome," says Russell Glass, who mines and sells consumer data. "People are afraid of what they really don't understand. They don't understand that companies like us have no idea who they are."[10] Glass adds that online advertisers usually have no interest in the most personal data of all—a customer's name.

> "It's the monster-under-the-bed syndrome. People are afraid of what they really don't understand."[10]
>
> —Russell Glass, CEO of Bizo, on why fears about consumer data mining are unfounded.

Online Advertising Pays for Free Content

A significant benefit of consumer data mining is that targeted advertising funds most of the free content available on the web. Just as television networks pay for the cost of producing shows by selling advertising time, many websites fund themselves either by selling advertising space or by selling their visitors' data to data mining companies. Google is the most prominent and successful example of a company that uses this business model. Google uses the consumer data it collects to power its advertising networks, and revenue from these advertising networks funds its many free services, such as Gmail, Google Earth, Google Books, and its ubiquitous search engine. Those free services attract more users, who provide more consumer data, and the circle continues.

Free content is not just provided by huge companies like Google. Smaller sites, such as blogs and wikis, contribute the bulk of the free information to the web, and they often use revenue from advertising to pay their costs. Harper believes that if web users stop providing data to these sites, targeted advertising will no longer work as a business model, and much of the web's free content will disappear. Harper notes that he would not be able to finance his government-transparency blog, *The WashingtonWatch.com*, without advertising revenue, which relies on user-supplied data. His site provides a valuable service to society by tracking and analyzing proposed federal legislation. "I add new features for my visitors when there is enough money to do it," he explains. "More money spent on advertising means more tools for American citizens to use across the web."[11]

New Products and Services

The power of commercial data mining can also be harnessed to create new products and services that benefit the individual and society as a whole. Some companies use the predictive power of data mining analytics to give their customers an edge. Dataminr uses data mining to predict movement in the stock market for its clients, and it can often do so in real time by predicting the effect of breaking news on various stocks and immediately sending its clients text messages. Google Analytics offers data mining itself as a service for companies that need help gathering and analyzing information about the effectiveness of their websites. Google also taps into its vast trove of data to offer free services that benefit the public. An example of this is Google Flu Trends, which tracks and analyzes web searches related to flu symptoms and treatments. Because people often research their flu symptoms online before visiting a doctor, Google Flu Trends is able to predict flu outbreaks days earlier than the Centers for Disease Control and Prevention.

Twitter has also become a very popular source of data for analysis. Companies like Crimson Hexagon sell sophisticated "listening software" that mines Twitter and other social media platforms for customer sentiment about various products. It relies on key words that convey emotion and complex algorithms that take into account the changing nature of sentiment in social media. Other companies offer free social media listening software that monitors simple sentiments, such as whether a product is popular or how the public feels about an organization like a sports team or a college. Many companies have made social media monitoring a key part of their business strategy.

Twitter data has also become a valuable source of information about events that need a response in real time, such as natural disasters. The Red Cross used Twitter data to monitor the effects of Hurricane Sandy in 2012 by analyzing the tweets of users in the affected area. The Red Cross was able to map areas without power and pinpoint locations that suffered from severe flood damage, which helped increase emergency response times. The United Nations also monitors Twitter and other social media data for indications of political and social unrest. This can be particularly helpful in identifying areas that are in need of humanitarian aid, since normal channels of communication in those areas are rarely reliable.

Online data mining offers unique insight into the ways individuals behave and interact with each other. Whether that knowledge is commercialized or used for public good, its benefits far outweigh any costs to personal privacy.

Commercial Data Mining Infringes on Consumers' Privacy

"Just as the Internet has opened up the world to each and every one of us, it has also opened up each and every one of us up to the world. And, increasingly, the price we're being asked to pay for all of this connectedness is our privacy."

—Gary Kovacs is the former CEO of Mozilla.

Gary Kovacs, *Tracking Our Online Trackers*, video, TED.com, February 2012. www.ted.com.

Consider these questions as you read:

1. How convincing is the argument that data mining invades individual privacy? Explain your answer.
2. Do you think that Target's practice of predicting whether a woman is pregnant and sending her ads for baby goods is an invasion of her privacy? Why or why not?
3. Does it worry you that your movements are being tracked online? Does this affect your opinion about the companies that are tracking you? Explain.

Editor's note: The discussion that follows presents common arguments made in support of this perspective, reinforced by facts, quotes, and examples taken from various sources.

The personal information that data mining uncovers is far more revealing than most people realize. Like a detective putting two and two together, data mining has the ability to make connections between disparate events. Privacy expert Daniel J. Solove calls this aggregation. Aggregation takes two or more pieces of data and combines them to make a prediction or draw a conclusion. According to Solove, this can reveal information that a person might want to keep private. He explains:

Suppose you bought a book about cancer. This purchase isn't very revealing on its own, for it indicates just an interest in the disease. Suppose you bought a wig. The purchase of a wig, by itself, could be for a number of reasons. But combine those two pieces of information, and now the inference can be made that you have cancer and are undergoing chemotherapy. That might be a fact you wouldn't mind sharing, but you'd certainly want to have the choice.[12]

Solove's example uses only two data points—a book purchase and a wig purchase. But as the number of data points increases, the amount that can be learned about an individual explodes exponentially. For instance, in a class project at the Massachusetts Institute of Technology, two students analyzed about four thousand Facebook profiles of fellow students. By data mining anonymized profile data and mapping associations with other Facebook members, the two students were able to predict with 78 percent accuracy whether or not a Facebook profile belonged to a gay male.

Predictive Analytics Spell Trouble

Before online shopping became popular, most retailers performed aggregate data analysis on information they collected from sales and store loyalty cards. However, even this simple form of data analysis can be so precise that it can actually alienate customers. Target learned this the hard way back in 2003 when it used the information it gathered from sales to target pregnant women. The company's data analytics department had found it could accurately identify pregnant women by mining purchase data and combining it with demographic information and general knowledge about pregnancy. As Charles Duhigg, who wrote about the incident in the *New York Times*, explains: "Take a fictional Target shopper named Jenny Ward, who is 23, lives in Atlanta and in March bought cocoa-butter lotion, a purse large enough to double as a diaper bag, zinc and magnesium supplements and a bright blue rug. There's, say, an 87 percent chance that she's pregnant and that her delivery date is sometime in late August."[13]

The problem was that Target did not take into account that pregnancy was a private matter. When the data mining program determined that a teenage girl was pregnant, it sent coupons for baby products to her home address. In the now famous incident, the girl's father stormed into the manager's office and demanded to know why Target was encouraging his daughter to have a baby. A short time later, he called the manager and apologized. His daughter was pregnant after all; she just had not told her family yet.

Even though this incident happened in 2003, it illustrates how intrusive data mining and analysis can be. A decade later, huge data brokerage companies like the Acxiom Corporation have moved from aggregate analytics (such as using multiple data points to determine that a woman is pregnant) to predictive analytics (such as predicting what a pregnant woman will buy in the future). Acxiom claims that it has detailed profiles on about 700 million consumers. "They load all this data into sophisticated algorithms that spew out alarmingly personal predictions about our health, financial status, interests, sexual orientation, religious beliefs, politics and habits,"[14] explains Julie Brill, a member of the Federal Trade Commission. The company uses these predictions to classify consumers into more than seventy detailed socioeconomic groups. An Acxiom investor presentation gave an example of one such socioeconomic group: the "savvy single." As the *New York Times* reported, a savvy single is upper-middle class, attends pro sporting events, banks online, and would be likely to respond to free shipping offers.

> "They load all this data into sophisticated algorithms that spew out alarmingly personal predictions about our health, financial status, interests, sexual orientation, religious beliefs, politics and habits."[14]
>
> —Julie Brill, member of the Federal Trade Commission, on the data brokerage firm Acxiom.

Acxiom also ranks consumers, classifying some as high-value prospects and others as "waste," an industry slang term for consumers who are unlikely to respond to marketing efforts. Privacy advocates like Pam Dixon, the executive director of the World Privacy Forum, worry that ranking consumers in this way discriminates against some of them by not

Hundreds of Advertisers Secretly Track a Typical User

Most people do not realize that hundreds of advertisers secretly track their movements online, collecting data and installing cookies on their computers. This visualization shows the advertisers that are tracking a user after only ten popular websites (such as google.com and facebook.com) are visited. These sites are shown as red circles. The blue circles represent websites the user has visited in the past (such as virginia.gov and craigslist.org) and the green triangles represent websites never visited by the user (such as trimedmedia.com and scorecardresearch.com). The image was created by Firefox's free add-on program Lightbeam.

A Visualization of Web Tracking

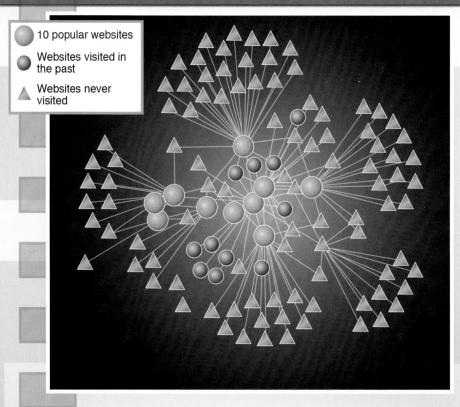

- 10 popular websites
- Websites visited in the past
- Websites never visited

Source: Christine Wilcox, Firefox Lightbeam, January 30, 2014. www.mozilla.org.

giving them equal access to discounts or services. "Over time, that can really turn into a mountain of pathways not offered, not seen and not known about,"[15] Dixon explains. Other experts worry that this form of predictive analytics will lead to other types of consumer ranking, such as a score that identifies customers who are likely to complain, return items, or write bad reviews online.

Huge data brokerage companies like Acxiom are not the only threats to privacy online. As computers become more sophisticated and data mining tools become more readily available, it becomes easier for identity thieves to use predictive analytics to mine public data for sensitive information. To illustrate this, two researchers from Carnegie Mellon University reported that, using only information publicly available online, they could predict the social security number of 8.5 percent—or nearly 5 million—of the individuals born between 1989 and 2003.

> "Imagine in the physical world if somebody followed our children around with a camera and a notebook, and recorded their every movement. . . . We'd take action."[16]
>
> —Gary Kovacs, former CEO of Mozilla, on online tracking of children.

Behavioral Tracking

One of the reasons that it is so difficult for individuals to fight back against the intrusive practices of aggregate and predictive analytics is that companies do not just collect the data provided when a person orders something on Amazon or shares something in a public Twitter post. Companies also track a user's movements online in a process called behavioral tracking. Behavioral tracking uses cookies—small files that are embedded into a user's computer when he or she visits a website—to track a user's movements around the web. A commercial site that has lots of ads on it might allow its advertising partners to upload fifty or more cookies to a user's computer, all without his or her permission.

To make this practice more transparent, Mozilla created a free add-on to its web browser, Firefox, called Lightbeam. Lightbeam visually shows which companies are tracking a user as he or she moves around on the Internet. In a presentation he made at the TED conference in 2012, then

CEO of Mozilla, Gary Kovacs, explained how he tested Lightbeam on himself on a typical day. After navigating to only four sites, Lightbeam revealed that more than 25 sites were tracking him. By the end of the day, that number had increased to more than 150 sites. His nine-year-old daughter, who navigated to principally children's sites, had the same experience. None of these sites had Kovacs's permission to track him or his family. He says, "Imagine in the physical world if somebody followed our children around with a camera and a notebook, and recorded their every movement. . . . We'd take action."[16] Kovacs hopes that tools like Lightbeam will help consumers fight back against behavioral tracking.

Privacy Is Not an Option

In his presentation, Kovacs makes the point that "privacy is not an option"[17] on the Internet. In this he is correct; there is currently no way to completely opt out of behavioral tracking and other data collection and data mining activities. Users can set their browsers to reject cookies, but this disables the functionality of many websites, which use cookies to help a site load faster or transact online purchases. Many browsers now come with Do Not Track settings, but these only let sites know that the user does not wish to be tracked. Websites are under no obligation to honor the user's wishes, and the ones that track a user's movements secretly will usually ignore this preference.

Finally, big companies like Google and Facebook are notorious for having convoluted privacy policies, changing them frequently, and sometimes ignoring them altogether. In November 2013 Google was fined $17 million for ignoring its own privacy policy and bypassing the privacy settings on Apple's Safari browser. Unlike other browsers, Safari's default setting blocks cookies, but Google exploited a loophole in the setting. Unfortunately, the fine probably will not do much to deter companies like Google from continuing these practices because, as the *New York Times* reported, a fine of $17 million is "just a tiny fraction of the billions of dollars that Google earns in advertising revenue each year."[18] As long as targeted advertising and the data mining that powers it is big business, privacy on the Internet will not exist.

Chapter Two

Should Online Privacy Be Sacrificed for National Security?

Some Online Privacy Must Be Sacrificed for National Security

- Online surveillance is the most powerful weapon the government has against terrorism.
- Within reason, most people value security over privacy.
- Laws are in place to protect the privacy of American citizens.

The Debate at a Glance

Online Privacy Should Not Be Sacrificed for National Security

- Online surveillance discourages free speech.
- Online surveillance creates a power imbalance between a government and its citizens.
- Online surveillance puts personal information at risk.

Some Online Privacy Must Be Sacrificed for National Security

"I think it's important to recognize that you can't have 100 percent security, and also then have 100 percent privacy and zero inconvenience. We're going to have to make some choices as a society."

—Barack Obama is the forty-fourth president of the United States.

Barack Obama, quoted in Tom McCarthy, "Obama Defends Secret NSA Surveillance Programs—as It Happened," *Guardian* (London), June 7, 2013. www.theguardian.com.

Consider these questions as you read:

1. What is the strongest argument for the view that some online privacy must be sacrificed to ensure national security? Explain your answer.
2. The essay argues that since metadata is not considered protected speech, collecting it does not violate personal privacy. Do you agree with this argument? Why or why not?
3. Are you willing to let the government collect and store your personal data if it might help prevent another terrorist attack? Explain your answer.

Editor's note: The discussion that follows presents common arguments made in support of this perspective, reinforced by facts, quotes, and examples taken from various sources.

In an age when it is possible for a handful of terrorists to kill thousands—or hundreds of thousands—of people, online privacy is not a luxury Americans can afford. After the 9/11 terrorist attacks, the US government dramatically increased its online surveillance capabilities so that it could monitor all communications between the United States and foreign nations. Even though this practice can infringe on personal privacy, it is still the best tool America has to prevent future terrorist attacks. The security gained through Internet surveillance far outweighs the costs to privacy.

Most People Value Security over Privacy

Sacrificing privacy for security is not a new practice. Even before the 9/11 terrorist attacks, Americans regularly allowed the government to infringe on their personal privacy. People have become accustomed to metal detectors at airports, bag searches at large events, and video cameras in public spaces. Americans are also aware that the post office can open and inspect suspicious packages and that police can read e-mails or listen to telephone calls if they first prove to a judge that there is a reasonable suspicion of criminal activity. All of these actions infringe on individual privacy, yet most people accept them as necessary to ensure the public's safety.

In fact, Americans have consistently prioritized security over privacy. The Pew Research Center conducted a poll of Americans from June 6 to 9, 2013—a time when the news was dominated by revelations that the NSA was collecting Internet metadata from American citizens. According to the poll, 62 percent of Americans surveyed still thought it was more important for the government to investigate terrorist threats than it was to respect personal privacy. Polls going back seven years have similar results, which indicates that the public has made up its mind about the issue. Although it is true that support for NSA surveillance dropped in late 2013, the drop coincided with news reports about specific abuses and violations within the NSA. This indicates that Americans believe that national security takes priority over privacy in principle, but that they oppose abuses of power within the government.

The NSA Is Not Reading E-mail

The government's Internet surveillance programs are actually less intrusive than more common and accepted infringements on privacy. Programs like PRISM, the NSA's main Internet data collection program, are designed to focus only on foreign targets, not on people within the United States. They also examine only the records that describe a user's online activity, not the activity itself. These records are known as metadata, or data about data. Some examples of metadata are online chat buddy lists, Internet browser histories, and the headings of e-mails. The courts have consistently ruled that metadata is not protected speech and that it is the property of the communication company, not the individual. In fact, the metadata the government collects usually comes directly from online companies like Facebook and Google, who collect it from their users with permission.

Sometimes the metadata generated by American citizens is collected along with metadata from foreign targets. This is because their metadata has been grouped together so that it can be mined, or analyzed, for patterns. As Deputy Attorney General James Cole explains, "If you're looking for the needle in a haystack, you have to have the haystack."[19] In other words, data mining is not effective unless all related metadata is included in the data set. Incomplete data sets are especially problematic when mapping associations between people—a crucial part of the NSA's antiterrorist efforts. When only a portion of the metadata is collected, missing links are likely and trails can go cold.

> "If you're looking for the needle in a haystack, you have to have the haystack."[19]
>
> —Deputy Attorney General James Cole, explaining that data mining only works on large data sets.

The reason that the government focuses on metadata rather than user-created data is that metadata is easily searchable. Metadata also reveals the context of online activities—where individuals are located, who they are talking with, what they are looking at online, when these activities are taking place, and so forth. For instance, if the NSA had intelligence that an IT worker in the Chicago area was making a bomb, a keyword search of a word such as *bomb* would turn up millions of e-mails. However, a search of the metadata might reveal that an e-mail from an IT company in Chicago was sent to an associate of a suspected terrorist in Pakistan. While this hypothetical example is simplistic, it illustrates that President Barack Obama's assurance that online surveillance programs "do not involve reading the e-mails of US citizens or US residents"[20] is simply common sense. In a world where more than 1,000 petabytes of information is carried over the Internet each day (1 petabyte = 1,000,000,000,000,000 bytes), any effort to monitor user-created content would be quickly overwhelmed.

National Security More Important than Online Privacy

After learning that the US government was surveilling the online activities of American citizens, the public still felt that national security was more important than personal privacy. This graph shows that the percentage of people who prioritized national security over personal privacy stayed about the same over a seven-year period. The final poll coincided with the breaking news report that the NSA was collecting the phone records and email contact lists of Americans.

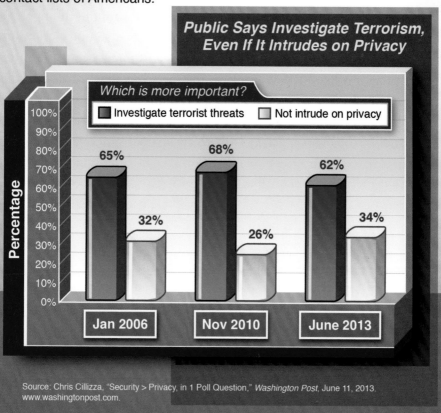

Public Says Investigate Terrorism, Even If It Intrudes on Privacy

Which is more important?

■ Investigate terrorist threats   □ Not intrude on privacy

Jan 2006: 65%, 32%
Nov 2010: 68%, 26%
June 2013: 62%, 34%

Source: Chris Cillizza, "Security > Privacy, in 1 Poll Question," *Washington Post*, June 11, 2013. www.washingtonpost.com.

A Powerful Early Warning System

One criticism of the government's online surveillance programs is that they have not yet prevented a terrorist attack. Even if this is true (and it may not be, since the NSA classifies most of its activities and cannot discuss them in the media), programs like PRISM still help keep the nation secure. According to an independent panel appointed by Obama, PRISM (which is also known as "702" because it is authorized by section 702 of the Foreign Intelligence Surveillance Act (FISA) Amendments Act of 2008) was found to be a valuable tool that has contributed greatly to national security. According to panel member and law professor Geoffrey Stone, "With 702, the record is very impressive. . . . It's no doubt the nation is safer and spared potential attacks because of 702."[21]

Online surveillance programs like PRISM are designed to fill the gaps in US intelligence capabilities, which 9/11 painfully brought to light. Before the terrorist attacks, the government had no way to monitor communications between the United States and foreign countries. But with programs like PRISM in place, the metadata attached to overseas Internet traffic is routinely searched for suspicious patterns of behavior. For instance, if a person visits a bomb-making website, that is not necessarily suspicious behavior—there are many legitimate reasons for researching explosives. But if that person was also chatting online with someone on an NSA watch list, PRISM can flag him or her for further investigation. This is exactly the type of intelligence that can stop a terrorist attack before it happens. According to former vice president Dick Cheney, "As everyone who's been associated with the programs [PRISM and similar programs] has said, if we had had this before 9/11 . . . we might well have been able to prevent 9/11."[22] In other words, if PRISM had been in place, it could very well have flagged the online communications between terrorists in the United States and those overseas.

Effective Oversight and Self-Reporting

The surveillance activities of the NSA are overseen by the FISA court, which makes sure that the NSA is not exceeding its powers. Even with this oversight, there is ample evidence that NSA self-monitors its activities rigorously and is committed to working within the law. For instance, in August 2013 the government declassified FISA court documents that showed that the NSA had been inadvertently collecting e-mails between Americans. Benjamin Wittes points out that it actually proves that the NSA monitors itself. He writes:

The story these documents tell . . . involves remarkable self-reporting by the executive branch [NSA]—both to the court and to the Congress. It involves a court that looks [nothing] like a rubber stamp. It involves a significant rebuke by that court to the government [NSA] both for the substance of its activities and for the accuracy of a series of representations it had made in the past. And it involves a swift effort by the government to correct the problem—one that within a few weeks the court accepted.[23]

Not only are there ample privacy protections for American citizens in the law, but the NSA has demonstrated that when it inadvertently oversteps its powers, it informs the FISA court and remedies the situation—in this case, by purging all relevant e-mails from its databases.

The United States must use every tool at its disposal to protect itself from terrorism. Online surveillance is key to that effort. "To date, we've not been able to come up with a better way of doing it," NSA director Keith Alexander explained to Congress, stating that abandoning bulk surveillance programs would be "an unacceptable risk to our country."[24]

> "To date, we've not been able to come up with a better way of doing it."[24]
>
> —NSA director Keith Alexander, on why mass online surveillance is critical to national security.

Online Privacy Should Not Be Sacrificed for National Security

"Spying and secrecy violate both our rights and our dignity. . . . [They] are both manifestations of, and further steps in the direction of, totalitarianism."

—Glen T. Martin is professor of philosophy and chair of the Peace Studies Program at Radford University in Virginia.

Glen T. Martin, "NSA Spying, Secrecy, and the Totalitarian Threat," OpEdNews.com, February 1, 2014. www.opednews.com.

Consider these questions as you read:

1. How does the essay support the argument that online surveillance by the government negatively affects free speech and a free press? Do you agree or disagree with this argument?
2. Describe one way that the essay argues that online surveillance by the government threatens democracy. Do you agree with the argument? Why or why not?
3. Can you think of a situation where you might not exercise your right to free speech because of online surveillance? Explain your answer.

Editor's note: The discussion that follows presents common arguments made in support of this perspective, reinforced by facts, quotes, and examples taken from various sources.

Many Americans believe that it is worth giving up some privacy for protection from terrorism—especially if one has nothing unlawful or embarrassing to hide. However, the "nothing to hide" argument does not take into account other ways in which online surveillance by the government can harm its citizens. Online surveillance inhibits free speech and free association, creates a power imbalance between citizens and their government, and puts democracy at risk. Taken together, the costs of online surveillance are not worth the modest gains to national security.

Threats to Free Speech and a Free Press

Because nearly all communication is vulnerable to online surveillance in the digital age, any evidence that the government is spying on its citizens will have the effect of suppressing free speech. The NSA claims that it does not target US citizens without a warrant. But documents leaked by Edward Snowden tell a different story. According to Snowden, "The vast majority of human communications are automatically ingested [processed and stored in NSA databases] without targeting."[25] Government documents support this, making it clear that at least some of the vast amounts of data the NSA has collected and stored belongs to American citizens. The problem is, people do not know whether their data has been collected. And each time one of the NSA's advanced surveillance techniques is reported in the news (such as the ability to take control of users' webcams remotely or the practice of intercepting new computers en route to customers and loading them with spyware), the public gets a little more paranoid. Citizens cannot speak freely when they know that everything they say might be recorded, stored, and perhaps used against them one day.

Not only is the average American going to think twice before criticizing the government online, but so will activists and whistleblowers. Gabriella Coleman, a professor of scientific and technological literacy at McGill University in Quebec, Canada, believes that online surveillance will curtail not just political activism but all forms of community organization. She explains that whether activist activity includes "organizing to set up a union at work or to challenge new abortion laws in your state, there is no reason why government should be surveilling this activity. And historically we know that when they collect [information] and surveil this activity it is used against activists all the time."[26]

Freedom of the press is also harmed by online surveillance. Although journalists are protected by the First Amendment, their sources are not. Even though a journalist cannot be forced by the government to reveal a source, the source's anonymity is not constitutionally protected. Journalists will have a harder time guaranteeing anonymity to their sources if those sources are worried that the government is monitoring the online activity of journalists. In this case simply the threat of government surveillance can erode the country's First Amendment right to a free press, which acts as a check against the power of the government.

No Defense Against Wrong Information

Even with these risks to free speech and a free press, some Americans are still willing to give up some of their privacy for national security. They often believe that if they have nothing to hide—if they are honest, law-abiding citizens—then they have nothing to fear from government surveillance. Privacy expert Daniel J. Solove points out that it is actually the secret nature of surveillance that can cause harm. When the government collects information about its citizens in secret, those citizens have no way to check the information for errors or to defend themselves against false accusations. "What if the government mistakenly determines that based on your pattern of activities, you're likely to engage in a criminal act?" Solove asks in his book *Nothing to Hide: The False Tradeoff Between Privacy and Security*. "What if the government leaks the information to the public? . . . What if it denies you the right to fly? What if the government thinks your financial transactions look odd—even if you've done nothing wrong—and freezes your accounts?"[27] Solove explains that when citizens are excluded from knowing what information the government has collected, they can feel helpless and powerless. This damages their relationship with institutions that are supposed to serve them.

No More Checks and Balances

Online surveillance does not harm just the individual; it harms the democratic system. Daniel Ellsberg, former US military analyst and leaker of the Pentagon Papers (which detailed secret US operations during the Vietnam War), is concerned that government surveillance by the executive branch will weaken the other two branches of government. He worries that the NSA—which is controlled by the executive branch of government—may also have access to the communications of judges and members of Congress. "I think it's very naïve to imagine that you can have separate branches of government," he says, "when one branch, the executive, knows the entire private life and private communications, conversations, of every member of the other branch."[28] In a governmental system built on checks and balances, free and private communication is essential.

Online surveillance also shifts the balance of power in favor of the reigning political party. The executive branch has a history of abusing the power of its intelligence agencies. Political opponents, union leaders, and activists have all come under government surveillance in the past. For instance, civil rights leader Martin Luther King Jr. was threatened with exposure after surveillance revealed he had been unfaithful to his wife, and the Watergate scandal of 1972 to 1974 revealed that President Richard Nixon was bugging the offices of his political opponents. Even without proof, the knowledge that the government may use surveillance against a group of people can intimidate them and inhibit their actions.

> "I think it's very naïve to imagine that you can have separate branches of government when one branch, the executive, knows the entire private life and private communications, conversations, of every member of the other branch."[28]
>
> —Daniel Ellsberg, former US military analyst.

A Threat to Democracy

Perhaps the greatest harm of prioritizing national security over personal privacy is that secret government surveillance puts democracy itself at risk. Former surveillance expert William Binney warned about this threat in 2001 after he resigned from the NSA. He claimed that after 9/11 the NSA began spying on American citizens with a powerful software program he had designed for foreign surveillance. Binney had built safeguards into the program to protect the privacy of any Americans who were inadvertently swept up by the system, but the NSA stripped them out. According to Binney, the NSA now has detailed profiles of the majority of Americans. This was confirmed by Edward Snowden in 2013, who told the *Guardian*, "If I wanted to see your e-mails or your wife's

Most Americans do not think it is worth giving up their privacy online to help fight terrorism. In January 2014, the American public's support of online data collection as a method of fighting terrorism fell to 40 percent. This graph shows that in the month after the initial reports of NSA surveillance, the public's support of national security efforts at the expense of online privacy increased slightly. However, that support fell as more details were reported in the news.

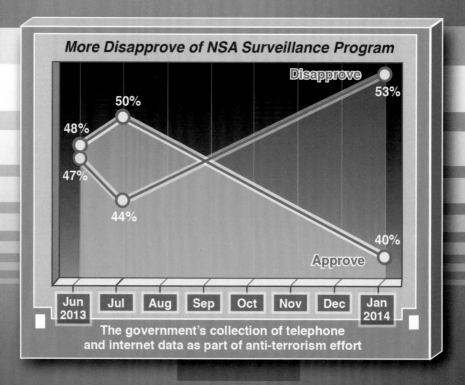

Source: Pew Research Center for the People and the Press, "Obama's NSA Speech Has Little Impact on Skeptical Public," The Pew Research Center, January 20, 2014. www.people-press.org.

phone, all I have to do is use intercepts. I can get your e-mails, passwords, phone records, credit cards."[29]

Binney and other NSA critics are concerned that having so much information about the private lives of American citizens gives the government far too much power. "The danger here is that we fall into something like a totalitarian state like East Germany," Binney explains. "Just because we call ourselves a democracy doesn't mean we will stay that way. And we the people will have absolutely nothing to say about it."[30]

Historically, when a government becomes too powerful it begins to equate itself with the country it serves. It then views itself—rather than the people it represents—as needing protection and defense. Glen T. Martin, chair of the Peace Studies Program at Radford University, thinks that this is beginning to happen in the United States. He believes the US government is using the threat of terrorism to justify using surveillance to gain power over its citizens. "Totalitarian regimes need enemies," he explains. "Hitler needed the 'Jewish conspiracy,' while Stalin needed 'subversives and decadents.' Our secretive . . . U.S. government claims that we are under terrorist threat and attack around the world, as assessed by secret criteria and supported by secret evidence."[31] Martin believes that if the government's surveillance activities are not reined in by the people, the United States will eventually cease to be a democracy.

Even if the terrorist threat is as grave as the government claims, in the years since 9/11, the NSA's online surveillance programs have not prevented a single terrorist attack. When that track record is coupled with the fact that the chance of being killed by a terrorist is about 1 in 20 million, it is hard to justify the NSA's intrusive and damaging online surveillance programs—programs that erode the very freedoms that the government is sworn to protect.

"If I wanted to see your e-mails or your wife's phone, all I have to do is use intercepts. I can get your e-mails, passwords, phone records, credit cards."[29]

—Former contractor Edward Snowden, on the information he had access to at the NSA.

Chapter Three

Do the Benefits of Electronic Health Records Outweigh Risks to Privacy?

Electronic Health Records Benefit the Individual and Society

- Electronic health records (EHRs) improve efficiency and save money.
- Electronic records vastly improve patient health outcomes.
- Patient portals empower patients and improve compliance.

The Debate at a Glance

Electronic Health Records Threaten Patient Privacy

- Too many entities have access to EHRs.
- There is already evidence that EHRs are not secure.
- Even if health records are made anonymous, patients can be identified.

Electronic Health Records Benefit the Individual and Society

"I think this is the last great hope for American medicine."

—Robert Pearl is executive director of Kaiser Permanente.

Quoted in Devin Leonard and John Tozzi, "Why Don't More Hospitals Use Electronic Health Records?," *Bloomberg Businessweek*, June 21, 2012, www.businessweek.com.

Consider these questions as you read:

1. How persuasive is the argument that the benefits of EHRs outweigh the privacy risks? Which argument provides the strongest support for this point of view, and why?
2. According to the essay, how do patient portals promote wellness?
3. If all other things were equal, would you prefer to visit a hospital that used an EHR system or one that used a paper-based system? Explain your answer. Would your answer change if you had an illness or condition you did not want anyone to know about?

Editor's note: The discussion that follows presents common arguments made in support of this perspective, reinforced by facts, quotes, and examples taken from various sources.

The United States spends about 18 percent of its gross domestic product on health care, almost twice as much as any other advanced economy. Health-care spending strains family budgets and costs taxpayers more than $1 trillion a year. In response to this crisis, the Obama administration is attempting to make health care more efficient by giving doctors incentives to convert to EHRs. Though privacy advocates are concerned that EHRs are less secure than paper records, the ability of EHR systems to cut costs and save lives far outweigh any privacy concerns.

Improves Efficiency and Cuts Costs

Dr. George Palma remembers when his hospital still relied on paper medical charts: "Every time a patient visited the office or hospital, their file had to be physically pulled from a storage space, transported, delivered, stamped and sorted all in one visit."[32] He writes in an article for *Becker's Hospital Review* that it was not unusual for a third of his charts to be unavailable, which wasted time and affected patient care. But when his hospital switched over to EHRs, records were available at all times. This saved money—in storage space, in human resources, and ultimately in costs to patients, who got better care.

EHR systems save money in countless ways, streamlining a complex, cumbersome, and costly system. The savings in time and human resources alone make EHR systems attractive to hospitals. EHR systems also track a patient's use of hospital resources, which is known as "capture." In a busy hospital, charges can often be overlooked, but in an EHR system, charges for testing, supplies, medications, and staff resources are captured automatically and charged to a patient's account with minimal input from health-care workers. EHR systems also have enhanced electronic communication features among providers and between provider and patient. As anyone who uses text messaging or e-mail can attest, the phone is often not the most efficient way to communicate, and most physicians appreciate saving the time spent playing phone tag with colleagues by communicating through their EHR system. Finally, since EHR systems are often accessed by mobile devices, all of these features are portable. This means that providers can access patient records when they are out of the office, which can save precious time in an emergency.

None of these cost-cutting and lifesaving benefits would be possible if EHR systems did not have a feature that paper records do not: Access is restricted by passwords. Password protection is a feature of all EHR sys-

> "Every time a patient visited the office or hospital, their file had to be physically pulled from a storage space, transported, delivered, stamped and sorted all in one visit."[32]
>
> —Dr. George Palma, discussing the procedure before electronic health records.

Few Doctor Say Patient Privacy Is a Problem with Electronic Health Records

Privacy and security fall low on the list of problematic features of EHRs. This graph illustrates the results of a poll given by EHR Intelligence, an online resource for news and information about EHR systems. When doctors were asked what they disliked about their EHR systems, only 25 percent cited patient privacy and security as a concern.

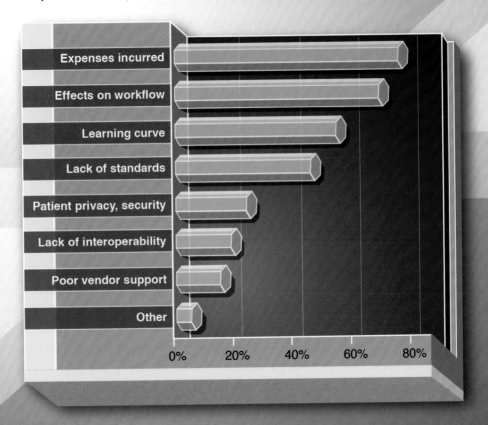

Source: Kyle Murphy, "Inpatient EHR Use Among Hospitals, Providers," EHR Intelligence, November 6, 2012. http://ehrintelligence.com.

tems. This added level of privacy protection ensures that only health-care professionals can view patient records. Password protection is also a far less cumbersome and costly security measure than the physical barriers necessary to protect paper records.

Lives Saved in the Emergency Room

EHR systems are especially effective in an emergency room setting, where they have helped vastly improve patient outcomes. For instance, when an elderly patient who was twitching uncontrollably was brought into an emergency room in California, the hospital's EHR system saved his life. The emergency room doctor thought the man was having an epileptic seizure and was about to send him to neurology, but his colleague first checked the hospital's EHR system. They immediately learned that the patient had a history of twitching episodes that were not characteristic of epilepsy. The doctor then determined the man was at risk of cardiac arrest and quickly transferred him to intensive care, where he was outfitted with a pacemaker. If the man's health records had not been immediately accessible, he might have died in neurology, where there was no equipment to diagnose a heart problem.

The hospital where this occurred was part of the Kaiser Permanente health system, a network of thirty-seven hospitals that has one of the largest nongovernmental EHR systems in the world. Kaiser's EHR system not only improves individual patients' outcomes by reducing errors and making records immediately available, but it also can be leveraged to improve overall health. For instance, EHRs can be data mined to find patients who have not scheduled necessary follow-up tests—something that is impossible to do with paper records. And at Kaiser, analysts examined data captured in the EHR system to reduce mortality rates for sepsis—a dangerous infection—by 40 percent. "We were able to go into our databases and understand the progression of this disease and recognize why early intervention is so crucial,"[33] explained Robert Pearl, executive director of Kaiser's Permanente Medical Group. According to Pearl, this would have been impossible without the EHR system, and lives would have been lost unnecessarily.

Cutting Costs by Focusing on Wellness

Small providers like Dr. Edward Rippel have had similar successes. Before Rippel moved to an electronic system, only 40 percent of his diabetic patients were keeping their blood sugar at a safe level. "I thought

I was doing a pretty good job," he said. "And it turns out that my percentage of success in getting patients to goal for diabetes was about the same as other primary care doctors in the United States. And I said, 'But that's not good enough.'"[34] Two years later that number increased to 70 percent. Rippel accomplished this by routinely contacting patients who were overdue for screening tests—something he could do through his EHR system in just a few minutes.

Part of the Affordable Care Act calls for health-care providers to use computers in the way Rippel does: as a tool to help shift their emphasis from diagnostic testing to wellness care. Most doctors have a financial incentive to order costly tests and procedures. The Affordable Care Act aims to rein in those costs by giving doctors an incentive to shift their focus to wellness. Using EHRs to improve patient compliance is one of the best ways to accomplish this. According to Judy Hanover, a health-care technology analyst, "You can't have the health-care reform act without electronic health records."[35]

> "You can't have the health-care reform act without electronic health records."[35]
>
> —Judy Hanover, health-care technology analyst.

Patient Portals

Another way EHRs promote wellness and reduce return trips to the doctor is by helping patients comply with their doctors' orders. EHRs do this through their patient portals. Patient portals allow patients to access their health records from a website, download test results, and schedule appointments. A feature that is especially popular with patients is the ability to e-mail their doctor or health-care team. Though many providers were at first worried that they would be inundated with e-mails from their patients, most report the system saves them time by allowing them to respond to patients at their convenience. Another feature that is popular with both patients and doctors is the clinical summary, which doctors can e-mail to patients via the patient portal or simply print out for them after their appointment. Doctors have found the clinical summary to be a great educational tool that improves compliance, especially with the elderly and patients who have multiple health conditions. A clinical summary will list medications, instructions, and information about follow-up appointments that can be shared with family members. According to health-care consultant Graham Brown, patient portals create "greater patient compliance, greater patient connection to a health care system, and greater responsibility for taking care of themselves,"[36] all key values necessary to any reform of health care in the United States.

EHR systems have already proved to be one of the most effective ways to improve patient outcomes and cut health-care costs. Although companies that provide EHR systems are relatively new to the technology industry and some have issues with functionality and security, their benefits far outweigh any risks to individual privacy.

Electronic Health Records Threaten Patient Privacy

"The impact is profound when there is a breach of health care information, which increasingly is being committed by people who know what they want. . . . Today, medical data are among the most sought-after data for committing fraud."

—Pam Dixon is executive director of the World Privacy Forum.

Quoted in Deborah L. Shelton, "Health Records Lost, Stolen or Revealed Online," *Chicago Tribune*, April 23, 2012. www.chicagotribune.com.

Consider these questions as you read:

1. Do you agree or disagree that the risks to privacy are too great to justify mandating that doctors and hospitals switch to EHR systems? Explain your answer.
2. Do you think the benefits to having a single sign-on process to an EHR system outweigh the risks to patient privacy? Why or why not?
3. Of the entities that may have legal access to your EHRs, which would make you the most uncomfortable? Explain your answer.

Editor's note: The discussion that follows presents common arguments made in support of this perspective, reinforced by facts, quotes, and examples taken from various sources.

By 2015 all US health-care providers must transition to EHRs or their federal Medicare reimbursements will be reduced. Because of this mandate, found in the American Recovery and Reinvestment Act of 2009, health-care providers are scrambling to bring their patient records into compliance. However, many do not have the knowledge or training to ensure that EHR systems are secure and that patient privacy is protected. Though EHR systems have the ability to improve patient care, a privacy breach can have a devastating effect on patients, exposing their most personal and private information to the world. The risk of a breach is simply too great to justify the use of EHRs.

Too Much Access

Doctors and hospitals are not the only entities that have access to EHR systems. Under the Affordable Care Act, the government has access to sensitive health information within EHR systems, which hospitals must use to report statistical information to the US Department of Health and Human Services. In addition, patient portals like Microsoft HealthVault can connect with EHRs so that patients can view their own health records. With so many entities having access to health records, the EHR systems must be well designed and have excellent security measures in place.

However, many EHR systems trade security for ease of use. For instance, because so many health-care workers need access to records, some EHR systems use a single sign-on process, giving all authorized health workers access to all records. This is the case with Sentara Healthcare, a system of eleven hospitals in Virginia and North Carolina. According to Ken Rice, director of system improvements, because the system has a single sign-on process, "we have terminated a lot of employees who have looked at their neighbor's or their ex-spouse's records."[37] Some EHR systems also cut corners by encouraging workers to use their own equipment. According to a survey of eighty health-care organizations, 81 percent allow workers to use their personal devices to connect with the EHR system, which leaves the system vulnerable to malware or other attacks and makes it easier for unauthorized users to access health records.

> "We have terminated a lot of employees who have looked at their neighbor's or their ex-spouse's records."[37]
>
> —Ken Rice, director of system improvements at Sentara Healthcare, on internal security breaches of his hospital's EHR system.

Because of these problems, many health-care professionals do not have confidence that their EHR systems are secure. According to two studies published in the *Journal of the American Medical Informatics Asso-*

ciation, 71 percent of physicians surveyed were concerned about possible privacy breaches of their EHR systems, and 83 percent of mental health–care professionals said that their patients did not want their records accessed by other health-care providers. "The thing I worry about is not that we are doing it, but that we're doing it without the right safeguards," said Lee Tien, a senior staff attorney with the Electronic Frontier Foundation. "We have been giving (medical providers) incentives to move into the electronic-health-records era. But we haven't been giving them enough guidance on how they're supposed to do it."[38]

Tien is concerned that medical data will not just be vulnerable to hackers and identity thieves, but also to pharmaceutical companies and entities that package and sell data profiles to advertisers. "Like any other kind of customer data, it gets bought and sold and you have no idea where it went,"[39] Tien said.

Problems Are Emerging

EHR systems are already fraught with security and design problems. As of April 2013, of the 77 percent of health-care providers that had moved to electronic records, 74 percent were not encrypting data on mobile medical devices, and only 21 percent scanned those devices for security issues before allowing them to connect to the network. And although nearly all EHR systems use cloud-based services to store data, 47 percent of health-care providers surveyed were not confident that data was secure in the cloud.

The systems are also being criticized for being poorly designed and causing recording errors. "Documenting a full clinical encounter in an EHR is pure torment,"[40] said Dr. Steven J. Stack, chair of the American Medical Association's board of trustees. To save time, doctors often cut and paste previous patient records into new forms—a practice that leads to inaccuracies, medical errors, and overpayments. In one incident, a patient who had a family history of breast cancer had her EHR changed to say that she personally had a history of breast cancer—a mistake caused by cutting and pasting from one part of her EHR to another. Because EHR systems are connected to so many entities, errors like these can be

Patient Privacy Breaches Are More Common with Electronic Records

It is more difficult to keep patients' medical records private when they are stored in an EHR system. Of 288 patient privacy breaches reported to the government over an 18-month period, 73 percent involved electronic data stored in an EHR system. More than half of those instances were due to theft or hacking.

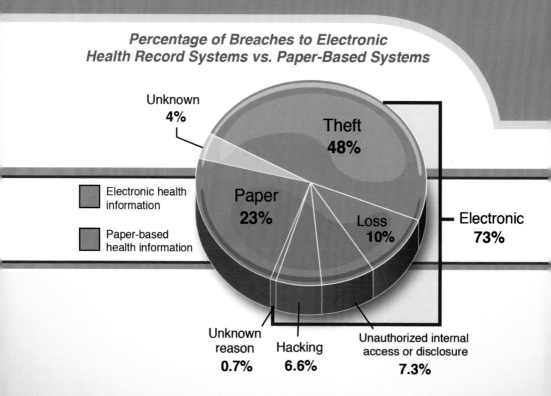

Percentage of Breaches to Electronic Health Record Systems vs. Paper-Based Systems

Unknown 4%

Theft 48%

Electronic health information

Paper 23%

Paper-based health information

Loss 10%

Electronic 73%

Unknown reason 0.7%

Hacking 6.6%

Unauthorized internal access or disclosure 7.3%

Source: Carrie Ghose, "Electronic Health Records Great but Vulnerable, PWC Study Finds," *Columbus* (OH) *Business First*, March 20, 2013. www.bizjournals.com.

very difficult to fix. "It goes through your system. It goes through other systems. It gets sent to other care providers; it gets sent to insurance companies," explained Diana Warner, director of the American Health Information Management Association. "We had to work for months to get that cleared up with the insurance company so her coverage would not be dropped."[41] If these records are stolen and sold before errors are corrected, the errors can follow a patient around for life, potentially affecting employment or making it impossible to get life insurance or long-term-care insurance.

Anonymity Can Be Broken

A similar worry surrounds records that are used for government research. To protect patient privacy, all identifying information in an EHR is usually deleted or altered before it is shared with researchers. The problem is that data mining software is becoming so powerful that it can reveal the identities of patients whose records have been made anonymous. For instance, Yaniv Erlich, a genetic researcher from the Massachusetts Institute of Technology, was able to uncover the identities of anonymous donors to the 1000 Genomes Project, whose genomes are freely available online for use in genetic research. Erlich cracked the billion-letter codes by matching them with genetic information found online in genealogy databases. He uncovered the identity of fifty individuals (he did not reveal the subjects' identities). According to Amy McGuire, a lawyer and ethicist at Baylor College of Medicine in Houston, "To have the illusion you can fully protect privacy or make data anonymous is no longer a sustainable position."[42]

> "We had to work for months to get that cleared up with the insurance company so her coverage would not be dropped."[41]
>
> —Diana Warner, director of the American Health Information Management Association, on the difficulties of correcting a simple error in a patient's EHR.

Significant Privacy Breaches

Many EHR systems have already been breached. Some privacy breaches are caused by unscrupulous health-care employees who take advantage of how easy it is to access information from an EHR system. For instance, in December 2013 it was discovered that a nurse working at the Riverside Health System in southeast Virginia had been stealing patient Social Security numbers for more than four years, violating the privacy of almost one thousand patients. Other breaches are perpetrated by hackers, such as the March 2012 theft of approximately 780,000 patient records from the Utah state government's servers, which received Medicaid information from multiple EHRs around the state. According to the Department of Health and Human Services, between 2009 and 2013 the security of 17,000 patient records was compromised in some fashion each day. Even though most of these breaches are inadvertent, it is estimated that 5 to 10 percent of them are incidents of theft by hackers, who go on to sell sensitive patient information to identity thieves.

EHR systems and the entities that have access to them are simply not secure enough. Until all of these security vulnerabilities are corrected—both within the government and within the health-care system—providers should not be required to use EHR systems.

Chapter Four

Are Stronger Protections Needed for Online Privacy?

Stronger Protections Are Needed for Online Privacy

- Corporations are not keeping personal data safe and are breaking their own privacy rules.
- Online privacy laws are outdated.
- Teenagers need special protection online.

The Debate at a Glance

Stronger Online Privacy Protections Are Unnecessary

- Internet users already have the ability to set privacy preferences.
- Lawmakers should not be responsible for protecting privacy online, because the legislative process moves too slowly to keep up with technological advances.
- Government regulations always have unintended consequences.

Stronger Protections Are Needed for Online Privacy

"Many of the best and most innovative sites and services on the web are available to users free of charge. Unfortunately, our privacy laws have not kept up with these changes and consumers are frequently and unknowingly paying for those innovations with their personal information and, inevitably, their privacy."

—Senator Al Franken is chair of the Judiciary Subcommittee on Privacy, Technology and the Law.

Al Franken, letter to the National Telecommunications and Information Administration, April 2, 2012. www.ntia.doc.gov.

Consider these questions as you read:

1. What is the strongest argument made in the essay that supports the idea that the government needs to pass more effective online privacy laws? Explain your answer.
2. What should be done about private companies that violate their own privacy policies?
3. Do you think teenagers should get special privacy protection online? Why or why not?

Editor's note: The discussion that follows presents common arguments made in support of this perspective, reinforced by facts, quotes, and examples taken from various sources.

A person needs only to scan the headlines to see that privacy on the Internet is under attack. Online companies are either being hacked or are ignoring their own privacy policies. The government is trying to enforce laws that were written before anyone had ever heard of the Internet. The American public is in dire need of stronger online privacy protections.

Corporations Are Not Keeping Customer Data Safe

In 2012 both the business networking site LinkedIn and the online dating site eHarmony were hacked, resulting in the theft of 8 million passwords—all of which were posted online. In 2013 the messaging site Snapchat—which uses privacy as its selling point by destroying user photos after a few seconds—was also hacked, and 4.6 million users had personal information posted online. And later that year, Target suffered one of the largest security breaches in history, resulting in millions of home addresses, telephone numbers, and credit card numbers being stolen. In Target's case the thieves got into the company's system through the Internet portal. Customers who had never even shopped online found their information stolen via the Internet, showing that online privacy and security issues do not apply just to online businesses—they apply to brick-and-mortar stores as well.

Despite their assurances about security, corporations do not seem to have the ability to keep private customer information safe. Senator Richard Blumenthal insists that "customers of companies have a right to expect that their private information will be properly safeguarded and secured."[43] However, there is no federal law that mandates that corporations even inform their customers of data breaches. That issue, like many others having to do with online privacy, has been left to the states to address. In fact, federal privacy laws are so unclear that the Federal Trade Commission—which is responsible for making sure businesses do not take advantage of their customers—may not have the legal authority to hold Target accountable for its 2013 data breach.

Corporations Are Breaking Their Own Privacy Rules

The law is also not clear about the penalties to a company when it is the one infringing on privacy. "Today there is no meaningful check on private-sector data collection," states Marc Rotenberg, president of the Electronic Privacy Information Center. "Companies post 'privacy policies' on websites and then do as they wish with the personal information they collect."[44]

Huge companies like Facebook and Google have been in the news dozens of times for infringing on their users' privacy rights, but often the law is on their side. For instance, in August 2013 a privacy group criticized Google for stating that it was not obligated to keep incoming e-mails from other e-mail providers private. Google was being sued for scanning content of incoming e-mails sent by people who did not use Gmail and using that data to drive its advertising—something it regularly does with the e-mails of Gmail users. "Just as a sender of a letter to a business colleague cannot be surprised that the recipient's assistant opens the letter, people who use web-based e-mail today cannot be surprised if their communications are processed by the recipient's ECS [electronic communication service] provider in the course of delivery,"[45] Google wrote in a court brief. In response, Rotenberg said, "It's alarming for the world's largest e-mail service provider to say that they don't have an obligation to protect privacy."[46] However, federal law still views e-mail as the property of the e-mail provider that sends or receives it, not of the person who wrote it, and Google has no obligation to keep its customers' incoming e-mails private. Unfortunately, the government has a strong incentive to keep the law the way it is: With no privacy law, e-mail can be easily accessed by police or the government without a warrant.

Online Privacy Laws Are Outdated

Privacy advocates like Senator Al Franken of Minnesota have been pushing for reforms to federal laws. "The groundwork I'd like to lay is that Congress is starting to keep pace with technology and how it impacts people's privacy,"[47] Franken said. In 2010 the Obama administration showed that it agreed privacy laws needed to be reformed when it submitted to Congress a Privacy Bill of Rights. However, as of this writing, Congress still has not taken up the legislation.

The reason privacy advocates have been pushing for new legislation is that the laws that apply to computer fraud and privacy issues were passed in 1986, before most people had even heard of the Internet. The result is that the laws are so vague that they criminalize what is now common on-line behavior. For instance, the Computer Fraud and Abuse Act (CFAA) makes it a crime to obtain information from a computer without authorization. Because the concept of authorization is not defined, it has been extended to include any online behavior that is not specifically authorized by a website. For instance, in 2013 hacker and activist Andrew Auernheimer was sentenced to three and a half years in prison for exposing a security loophole in AT&T's website that gave anyone free access to customers' e-mail addresses. To make a point, Auernheimer downloaded 114,000 e-mail addresses and told journalists about his discovery. Even though he did not release the e-mail addresses, and even though the information was freely available, a jury found that Auernheimer had broken the law because he did not have authorization to access the information.

> "Companies post 'privacy policies' on websites and then do as they wish with the personal information they collect."[44]
>
> —Marc Rotenberg, president of the Electronic Privacy Information Center.

His supporters claim that Auernheimer was being punished for his reputation as a hacker. But as technology writer Hanni Fakhoury points out, interpreting the law in this way also benefits corporations enormously. "Placing publicly available data within the purview of the CFAA allows *companies*—not the normal legislative process—to dictate what is and isn't criminal behavior,"[48] she writes. It also allows AT&T to avoid being blamed for the security problem that allowed the data to be accessed in the first place.

Teens Need Protection

Even if the federal government is unable or unwilling to pass comprehensive online privacy legislation, it must at least follow the lead of states like California and pass laws protecting the online privacy of teenagers. The federal law that currently protects children does not apply past the age of thirteen—the age when many young teens are getting involved in social media. Children are fifty-one times more likely than adults to be victims of identity theft, and most kids do not know how to protect their privacy when they first go online. For instance, when Scott Fitzsimones

Parents Concerned About Teens' Safety and Privacy Online

Parents do not think that their teens' privacy is adequately protected online. This was revealed in a 2013 survey by the Pew Research Center of over eight hundred parents of teenagers. When asked what worried them about their teens online, 81 percent were concerned (either "very concerned" or "somewhat concerned") that their teens' personal information was being collected by advertisers.

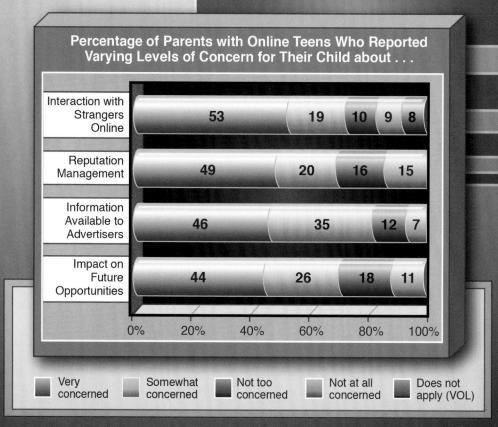

Percentage of Parents with Online Teens Who Reported Varying Levels of Concern for Their Child about . . .

	Very concerned	Somewhat concerned	Not too concerned	Not at all concerned	Does not apply (VOL)
Interaction with Strangers Online	53	19	10	9	8
Reputation Management	49	20	16	15	
Information Available to Advertisers	46	35	12	7	
Impact on Future Opportunities	44	26	18	11	

Source: Mary Madden et al., "Parents, Teens, and Online Privacy," Pew Internet & American Life Project, November 20, 2012. www.pewinternet.org.

got an iPhone for his thirteenth birthday, he immediately began setting up accounts and downloading apps with no thought to privacy. He told the *Washington Post* that when an app asks if it can track him, "I never say no. It's more annoying than anything when they ask, but I'm used to it now."[49] Experts claim that teens do not have the ability to make measured decisions about the information they share or to recognize the potential consequences of putting it online. According to Kathryn Montgomery, a privacy advocate and communications professor at American University, "Their ability to make decisions is still forming and clearly different from that of adults."[50]

To remedy this, Senator Edward Markey of Massachusetts introduced the Do Not Track Kids Act of 2013, which was strongly supported by Franken and other privacy advocates. Do Not Track Kids extended current privacy laws to teenagers, which mandates that companies keep kids' data secure and not track them for advertising purposes. "We must not allow the era of big data to become a big danger for children on the Internet in the 21st century," Markey said in a statement. "It is time for Congress to take action to ensure that children and teens are fully protected when they go online and parents have the tools they need to protect their kids."[51] However, Do Not Track Kids was unpopular with Republicans and was referred to committee for further discussion. The website GovTrack.us claims Do Not Track Kids has a 1 percent chance of being enacted. Unless the federal government partners with the online business community to make measured, comprehensive online privacy reform, citizens will continue to have their private information stolen, mined, and sold. As philosopher Helen Nissenbaum explains, "We really are in dire need of meaningful rules to level the playing fields, so that the values to which we subscribe—as societies, as cultures, as communities—can continue to be maintained."[52]

> "It is time for Congress to take action to ensure that children and teens are fully protected when they go online and parents have the tools they need to protect their kids."[51]
>
> —Senator Edward Markey of Massachusetts, in support of the Do Not Track Kids Act of 2013.

Stronger Online Privacy Protections Are Unnecessary

"The Internet is not for couch potatoes. It is an interactive medium. While Internet users enjoy its offerings, they should be obligated to participate in watching out for themselves."

—Jim Harper is director of information policy studies at the Cato Institute, a public policy research organization.

Jim Harper, "Economist Debates: Online Privacy: The Opposition's Opening Remarks," *Economist*, August 25, 2010. www.economist.com.

Consider these questions as you read:

1. Of the arguments presented against regulation of the Internet to protect online privacy, which is the strongest? Explain your answer.
2. Are the arguments in support of the idea that Internet users do not want more regulation convincing? Why or why not?
3. Do you think it is worth sacrificing your privacy for the free content available to you on the Internet? Why or why not?

Editor's note: The discussion that follows presents common arguments made in support of this perspective, reinforced by facts, quotes, and examples taken from various sources.

What differentiates the Internet from television—and what makes it infinitely more useful—is that the Internet is interactive. Every time a user types a keystroke or clicks a mouse, there is a server somewhere recording and acting on that information. Because the Internet works this way, there is no such thing as true privacy online. While people are entitled to expect that companies do their best to honor their privacy policies, any effort to regulate the Internet just makes it less dynamic and less useful. Instead of industry or government subjecting the entire Internet to more rules and regulations, privacy protection should be initiated by the individual and tailored to his or her own comfort level.

Why Do People Not Use Privacy Tools?

For people who are especially concerned about privacy, there are anonymous browsers and encryption services that even the NSA cannot crack. But even average users can do a great deal to keep their information private—from using secure passwords to taking the time to understand privacy policies before agreeing to them. However, most casual users do not take even these steps to protect themselves. For instance, all major Internet browsers have the ability to block cookies, which prevents most advertisers from using behavioral tracking and targeted ads. Yet most users do not change their browser settings to limit or reject cookies.

Privacy advocates sometimes assume that these people are simply ignorant and need to be protected, which is why Apple's Safari browser is now shipped with its default set to block third-party cookies. However, Jim Harper believes that Apple is missing the point. "The social engineer takes consumer indifference as a signal that people should be forced to prioritize privacy, but this would undercut consumer welfare as indicated by the best evidence available: consumer behavior," he explains. "People appear generally to prefer the interactivity and convenience of today's web, and the free content made more abundant by ad network tracking."[53] In other words, people do not block cookies because doing so limits interactivity. And if they did, websites would not get as much ad revenue, and free content would disappear.

There is evidence of this phenomenon in social media. According to a survey by the Internet marketing company Marketo, 13 million Facebook users have never touched their privacy settings, and almost a third of them deliberately share their posts with people they do not know. This is not because of ignorance about privacy. For instance, the people who society thinks need the most privacy protection—teenagers, who are too old to benefit from the Children's Online Privacy Protection Act (COPPA) but are supposedly too young to have good judgment—tend to be more savvy about privacy settings than adults. A recent survey by the Pew Internet &

American Life Project found that 89 percent of teen Facebook users say it is either "not difficult at all" or "not too difficult"[54] to manage Facebook privacy controls. Instead of worrying about privacy settings, teens spend a great deal of time crafting their social media persona, carefully deciding what to include and what to omit. In fact, 26 percent say that they deliberately post false information to protect their privacy. Daniel Sieberg, author of *The Digital Diet*, agrees with this strategy. He thinks that individuals should pay attention to what they share online instead of relying on corporations to shield their personal information from prying eyes. "What we choose to share or consume through social networks is a choice," he writes. "Sounds simple, but sometimes we seem to forget that concept."[55]

> "What we choose to share or consume through social networks is a choice. Sounds simple, but sometimes we seem to forget that concept."[55]
>
> —Daniel Sieberg, author of *The Digital Diet*.

Laws Cannot Protect Online Privacy

Privacy advocates like philosopher Helen Nissenbaum argue that, because it is nearly impossible to function in society without using the Internet, the government should regulate the Internet like a public utility. However, the government has proved itself to be very poorly equipped to craft meaningful and effective laws that protect online privacy—which may be why it has been so reluctant to do so since the mid-1980s, the last time major legislation related to online privacy was passed. As Cato Institute's Julian Sanchez points out, "By the time the courts get around to considering the appropriateness of some new method of technological surveillance, the technology has moved on."[56]

This became apparent in 2013, when the Federal Trade Commission fined Google $17 million for bypassing web browser Safari's privacy settings and installing cookies on millions of computers. In the two years it took for the Federal Trade Commission to settle the case, a new tracking method called device fingerprinting was developed, which makes the need for cookies obsolete. (Device fingerprinting identifies a computer

Many People Fail to Protect Their Privacy Online

Some people argue that more privacy protections online are unnecessary because most people do not use existing privacy tools. This graph shows that less than half of Internet users surveyed set their browsers to disable cookies, and only 14 percent used encryption or private web browsing services. In fact, most voluntarily shared identifying information including traceable e-mail addresses and usernames.

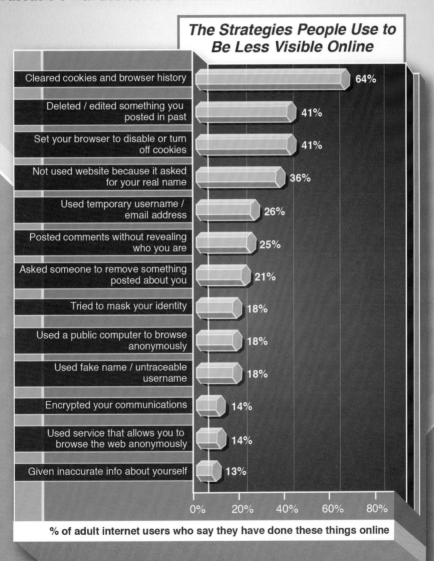

The Strategies People Use to Be Less Visible Online

Strategy	%
Cleared cookies and browser history	64%
Deleted / edited something you posted in past	41%
Set your browser to disable or turn off cookies	41%
Not used website because it asked for your real name	36%
Used temporary username / email address	26%
Posted comments without revealing who you are	25%
Asked someone to remove something posted about you	21%
Tried to mask your identity	18%
Used a public computer to browse anonymously	18%
Used fake name / untraceable username	18%
Encrypted your communications	14%
Used service that allows you to browse the web anonymously	14%
Given inaccurate info about yourself	13%

% of adult internet users who say they have done these things online

Source: Lee Rainie et al., "Anonymity, Privacy, and Security Online," Pew Internet & American Life Project, September 5, 2013. www.pewinternet.org.

by the unique way that it interacts with the Internet.) Technology writer Ben Richmond points out that "because regulations in the US and Europe limit cookies, advertisers can use fingerprinting as a legal loophole."[57] In other words, until the government changes the law again, Google can continue to legally track Safari users with device fingerprinting.

Regulations Have Unintended Consequences

When government does create legislation to protect online privacy, the laws often do little good—and sometimes do harm. An example of this is the push to extend COPPA protections to include those up to age sixteen. California passed such a bill, and the federal Do Not Track Kids bill of 2013 (which was still being discussed in congressional committee as of spring 2014) attempts to do the same thing. However, both the new California law and the federal bill cause more problems than they solve. For instance, one way that COPPA protects the online privacy of children up to age thirteen is by insisting parents give children permission to disclose personal information. But the Constitution gives teens the right to access information without their parents' permission, so extended COPPA rules have to be slightly different according to the age of the user. With two sets of rules, things get complicated, and ultimately the consumer suffers. Emma Llansó, director of the Center for Democracy & Technology's Free Expression Project, explains that having two sets of rules

> "By the time the courts get around to considering the appropriateness of some new method of technological surveillance, the technology has moved on."[56]
>
> —Privacy advocate Julian Sanchez of the Cato Institute.

incentivizes operators [website owners] either to collect more information about age or date-of-birth from all of their users, or—as we've seen with COPPA's under-13 category—to simply prohibit users in the defined age group from using the site or service. Neither of these outcomes is beneficial to the privacy . . .

rights of users of any age, which makes it difficult to justify these kinds of age-based regulations.[58]

In other words, under these laws, websites would have to collect more personal information from users, not less, and sites that find this too burdensome will simply deny access to all young people.

"Right to Know" Laws Would Hurt Businesses

Even though California has been taking the lead in enacting online privacy legislation, most of its new online privacy laws only protect small groups or target special issues. Like the federal government, California has been unable to pass more sweeping protections. For instance, a proposed "Right to Know" law was blocked in 2013 by lobbyists because it would have required all businesses to give customers a copy of their personal information on request and let them know with which third parties they had shared that information. "'Right to know' is an example of something that's not workable," says lawyer Jim Halpert, who represents a coalition that includes Amazon, Facebook, and Verizon. "It covers such a broad range of disclosures. We advocated against it."[59] Complying with the law would have been nearly impossible for large Internet companies that engage in behavioral tracking or online advertising.

Perhaps the strongest argument against an increase in online privacy protection—either by corporations or by the government—is that, despite what privacy advocates say, the public does not seem to object to behavioral tracking. According to the *Wall Street Journal*, Google—the same corporation that was fined $17 million for illegally spying on Safari users—posted a 17 percent increase in ad revenue in the fourth quarter of 2013, earning $14.1 billion that year. "Driving the increase in ad revenues was a 31 percent growth in clicks on the company's search advertisements,"[60] says reporter Rolfe Winkler. It seems that consumers are voting with mouse clicks—against more protections and in favor of the benefits of targeted advertising.

Source Notes

Overview: Online Privacy

1. Quoted in Janet Reitman, "Snowden and Greenwald: The Men Who Leaked the Secrets," *Rolling Stone*, December 4, 2013. www.rolling stone.com.

2. *Merriam-Webster*, "Data Mining," 2014. www.merriam-webster .com.

3. Dennis Kügler, "The Online Privacy Debate: Understanding the Basics," IVPN, May 17, 2013. www.ivpn.net.

4. Quoted in Timothy B. Lee, "Another E-mail Service Shuts Down over Government Spying Concerns," *The Switch* (blog), *Washington Post*, August 9, 2013. www.washingtonpost.com.

5. Quoted in Devin Henry, "Franken Takes Facebook to Task over Photo Tagging," *MinnPost*, July 19, 2012. www.minnpost.com.

6. Jaron Lanier, "How Should We Think About Privacy?," *Scientific American*, November 2013. www.scientificamerican.com.

Chapter One: Do the Benefits of Commercial Data Mining Outweigh the Risks to Privacy?

7. Andrew Cherwenka, "Expert Marketing Predictions: Is 2014 the Year of Personalization?," *Huffington Post*, January 6, 2014. www.huffing tonpost.com.

8. Michael Leander, "CircleTie First Mobile Location Based Advertising Solution in the Middle East and Egypt," *Mobile Marketing* (blog), Michael Leander Direct Marketing Consulting & Speaking, January 1, 2013. www.michaelleander.me.

9. Jim Harper, "Get Over Your 'Privacy' Concerns," *New York Times*, December 12, 2012. www.nytimes.com.

10. Quoted in Joel Stein, "Data Mining: How Companies Now Know Everything About You," *Time*, March 10, 2011. http://content.time.com.

11. Jim Harper, "It's Modern Trade: Web Users Get as Much as They Give," *Wall Street Journal*, August 7, 2010. http://online.wsj.com.

12. Daniel J. Solove, "Why Privacy Matters Even If You Have 'Nothing to Hide,'" *Chronicle of Higher Education*, May 15, 2011. http://chronicle.com.

13. Charles Duhigg, "How Companies Learn Your Secrets," *New York Times*, February 16, 2012. www.nytimes.com.

14. Julie Brill, "Demanding Transparency from Data Brokers," *Washington Post*, August 15, 2013. www.washingtonpost.com.

15. Quoted in Natasha Singer, "Mapping, and Sharing, the Consumer Genome," *New York Times*, June 16, 2012. www.nytimes.com.

16. Gary Kovacs, *Tracking Our Online Trackers*, video, TED.com, February 2012. www.ted.com.

17. Kovacs, *Tracking Our Online Trackers*.

18. Claire Cain Miller, "Google to Pay $17 Million to Settle Privacy Case," *New York Times*, November 18, 2013. 2013. www.nytimes.com.

Chapter Two: Should Online Privacy Be Sacrificed for National Security?

19. Quoted in Dana Bash and Tom Cohen, "Officials Cite Thwarted Plots, Oversight in Defending Surveillance," CNN, June 19, 2013. http://edition.cnn.com.

20. Quoted in White House, "Statement by the President," press release, June 7, 2013. www.whitehouse.gov.

21. Quoted in Michael Isikoff, "NSA Program Stopped No Terror Attacks, Says White House Panel Member," NBC News, December 20, 2013. http://investigations.nbcnews.com.

22. Quoted in Michael O'Brien, "Cheney Says NSA Monitoring Could Have Prevented 9/11," NBC News, June 16, 2013. http://firstread.nbcnews.com.

23. Benjamin Wittes, "The NSA Documents, Part I: Introduction," *Lawfare* (blog), August 22, 2013. www.lawfareblog.com.

24. Keith Alexander, "As Delivered Opening Remarks of General Keith Alexander, Director of the National Security Agency," IC On the Record, December 11, 2013. http://icontherecord.tumblr.com.

25. Quoted in Ewen MacAskill, "Edward Snowden, NSA Files Source: 'If They Want to Get You, in Time They Will,'" *Guardian* (London), June 9, 2013. www.theguardian.com.

26. Quoted in Brian Knappenberger, "Why Care About the NSA?," *New York Times*, November 25, 2013. www.nytimes.com.

27. Daniel J. Solove, *Nothing to Hide: The False Tradeoff Between Privacy and Security*. New Haven, CT: Yale University Press, 2011, p. 31.

28. Quoted in Knappenberger, "Why Care About the NSA?"

29. Quoted in MacAskill, "Edward Snowden, NSA Files Source."

30. Quoted in Laura Poitras, "The Program," *New York Times*, August 22, 2012. www.nytimes.com.

31. Glen T. Martin, "NSA Spying, Secrecy, and the Totalitarian Threat," OpEdNews.com, February 1, 2014. www.opednews.com.

Chapter Three: Do the Benefits of Electronic Health Records Outweigh Risks to Privacy?

32. George Palma, "Electronic Health Records: The Good, the Bad and the Ugly," *Becker's Hospital Review*, October 14, 2013. www.beckershospitalreview.com.

33. Quoted in Devin Leonard and John Tozzi, "Why Don't More Hospitals Use Electronic Health Records?," *Bloomberg Businessweek*, June 21, 2012. www.businessweek.com.

34. Quoted in Arielle Levin Becker, "A Hamden Doctor Explores the Changing Medical Landscape on His Own," *Connecticut Mirror*, June 20, 2011. http://ctmirror.org.

35. Quoted in Leonard and Tozzi, "Why Don't More Hospitals Use Electronic Health Records?"

36. Quoted in Ken Terry, "Patient Portal Explosion Has Major Health Care Implications," iHealthBeat, February 12, 2013. www.ihealthbeat.org.

37. Quoted in Neil Versel, "Taking a Close Look at Electronic Health Records," *U.S. News & World Report*, November 5, 2013. http://health.usnews.com.

38. Quoted in Jonathan Serrie, "ObamaCare Reg on Digital Patient Records Raises Security Concerns," Fox News, October 2, 2013. www.foxnews.com.

39. Quoted in Serrie, "ObamaCare Reg on Digital Patient Records Raises Security Concerns."

40. Quoted in Tom Sullivan, "AMA: EHRs Create 'Appalling Catch-22,'" Healthcare IT News, May 3, 2013. www.healthcareitnews.com.

41. Quoted in Erin McCann, "CMS Called Out for EHR Fraud Failings," Healthcare IT News, January 9, 2014. www.healthcareitnews.com.

42. Quoted in Gina Kolata, "Web Hunt for DNA Sequences Leaves Privacy Compromised," *New York Times*, January 17, 2013. www.nytimes.com.

Chapter Four: Are Stronger Protections Needed for Online Privacy?

43. Quoted in Kate Tummarello and Julian Hattem, "Target's Data Breach Sparks Calls for Action," *Hillicon Valley* (blog), *Hill* (Washington, DC), January 5, 2014. http://thehill.com.

44. Marc Rotenberg, "Economist Debates: Online Privacy, the Proposer's Opening Remarks," *Economist*, August 25, 2010. www.economist.com.

45. Quoted in Ian Munroe, "Google Lawsuit Stirs Debate over E-mail Privacy Rights," CBC News, August 16, 2013. www.cbc.ca.

46. Quoted in Munroe, "Google Lawsuit Stirs Debate over E-mail Privacy Rights."

47. Quoted in Devin Henry, "Franken Focuses In on Data Privacy as Technology Takes Off," *MinnPost*, December 15, 2011. www.minnpost.com.

48. Hanni Fakhoury, "You May Not Like Weev, but Your Online Freedom Depends on His Appeal," *Wired*, July 2, 2013. www.wired.com.

49. Quoted in Cecilia Kang, "Parting with Privacy with a Quick Click," *Washington Post*, May 8, 2011. www.washingtonpost.com.

50. Quoted in Kang, "Parting with Privacy with a Quick Click."

51. Quoted in Andrew Couts, "Facebook Won't Like This New Teenager Privacy Bill," Digital Trends, November 15, 2013. www.digitaltrends.com.

52. Quoted in Knappenberger, "Why Care About the NSA?"

53. Jim Harper, "Economist Debates: Online Privacy, the Opposition's Opening Remarks," *Economist*, August 25, 2010. www.economist.com.

54. Quoted in Mary Madden et al., "Teens, Social Media, and Privacy," Pew Internet & American Life Project, May 21, 2013. www.pewinternet.org.

55. Quoted in Todd Leopold, "Privacy? Forget It, We're All Celebrities Online Now," CNN, June 12, 2013. www.cnn.com.

56. Quoted in Knappenberger, "Why Care About the NSA?"

57. Ben Richmond, "How 'Device Fingerprinting' Tracks You Without Cookies, Your Knowledge, or Consent," *Motherboard* (blog), October 10, 2013. http://motherboard.vice.com.

58. Emma Llansó, "Do Not Track Kids Bill Revives Minors' Online Privacy Debate," Center for Democracy & Technology, November 26, 2013. www.cdt.org.

59. Quoted in Somini Sengupta, "No U.S. Action, so States Move on Privacy Law," *New York Times*, October 30, 2013. www.nytimes.com.

60. Rolfe Winkler, "Google Reports Higher Profit," *Wall Street Journal*, January 30, 2014. http://online.wsj.com.

Online Privacy Facts

Threats to Privacy Online

- More than 2 billion people—about 30 percent of the world's population—use the Internet, and 60 percent of them access the Internet every day.
- Sixty-five percent of Internet users are affected by online security threats like viruses and identity theft.
- There are approximately 3.1 trillion e-mail accounts registered on the Internet. Eighty-one percent of the e-mails sent to these accounts are spam.
- Twenty-one percent of Internet users have had their e-mail account or social networking profile hacked.
- Eleven percent of Internet users have had personal information stolen on the Internet.

Protecting Privacy Online

- Eighty-six percent of Internet users have taken steps to protect their privacy online.
- Sixty-eight percent of Internet users believe current laws are not good enough at protecting people's privacy online.
- Forty-one percent of US adults have uninstalled an app in order to protect their online privacy.
- Fifty-nine percent of Internet users do not believe it is possible to be completely anonymous online.

Teens and Privacy Online

- Of teenagers who have profiles on social media sites like Facebook, 91 percent post a photo of themselves, 71 percent post their school name and the city or town where they live, 53 percent post their e-mail address, and 20 percent post their cell phone number.

- Among teens with Facebook profiles, 14 percent have a public profile. Among teens with Twitter profiles, 64 percent have a public profile.
- Thirty-three percent of teenagers are friends on Facebook with people they have never met in person. This does not include public figures like celebrities, musicians, or athletes.
- Forty-four percent of teenagers on the Internet admit to lying about their age to circumvent a website's privacy rules.
- Fifty-six percent of millennials use a password or PIN to access their smartphones, compared to 36 percent of those aged thirty-five or older.
- Seventy-one percent of teenagers have asked for advice about how to ensure online privacy, 41 percent of them from their parents.

Government Surveillance Online

- According to NSA documents released by former contractor Edward Snowden:
    - The NSA data storage center in Utah has an estimated data capacity of 5 zettabytes, the equivalent of 1.5 trillion DVDs.
    - The NSA collects contact information from an estimated five hundred thousand buddy lists on live chat services each day.
    - The NSA is investing $80 million in software that will break every kind of encryption used to secure banking, medical, business, and government data.
    - The NSA has installed spyware on more than fifty thousand computer networks worldwide.
    - An internal NSA audit performed in May 2012 found 2,776 incidents in the previous year where the NSA had broken privacy rules. Each incident involved up to 3,032 files.

Related Organizations and Websites

American Civil Liberties Union (ACLU)
125 Broad St., 18th Floor
New York, NY 10004
phone: (212) 549-2500
e-mail: media@aclu.org
website: www.aclu.org

One goal of the ACLU is to protect civil liberties online. Its website contains general information and statistics about online privacy, as well as information about laws, court decisions, and ACLU activities and campaigns.

Cato Institute
1000 Massachusetts Ave. NW
Washington, DC 20001
phone: (202) 842-0200
website: www.cato.org

The Cato Institute is a public policy think tank that conducts research on policy issues affecting individual liberty, limited government, free markets, and peace. Its website contains publications and information about online privacy issues.

Center for Safe and Responsible Internet Use
474 W. Twenty-Ninth Ave.
Eugene, OR 97405
phone: (541) 556-1145
e-mail: contact@csriu.org
website: www.cyberbully.org

The Center for Safe and Responsible Internet Use helps young people keep themselves safe and respect others on the Internet. Its website contains information designed to help people learn about responsible Internet behavior.

Electronic Frontier Foundation (EFF)
454 Shotwell St.
San Francisco, CA 94110
phone: (415) 436-9333
e-mail: information@eff.org
website: www.eff.org

The EFF is a nonprofit organization that defends civil liberties in relation to telecommunications technologies such as the Internet. Its website has information about free speech and privacy issues related to Internet use.

Electronic Privacy Information Center (EPIC)
1718 Connecticut Ave. NW, Suite 200
Washington, DC 20009
phone: (202) 483-1140 • fax: (202) 483-1248
website: www.epic.org

EPIC is a public interest research center in Washington, DC. It was established in 1994 to focus public attention on emerging civil liberties issues and protect privacy, the First Amendment, and constitutional values. Its website contains information about policy issues in the electronic age, including privacy online.

GetNetWise
e-mail: cmatsuda@neted.org
website: www.getnetwise.org

GetNetWise is a website provided by Internet industry corporations and public interest organizations. Its goal is to ensure that Internet users have safe and constructive online experiences. The website contains information about youth safety, security, and privacy.

Pew Internet & American Life Project
1615 L St. NW, Suite 700
Washington, DC 20036
phone: (202) 419-4500 • fax: (202) 419-4505
e-mail: info@pewinternet.org
website: http://pewinternet.org

The Pew Internet & American Life Project studies how Americans use the Internet and how digital technologies are shaping the world today. Its website has the results of numerous studies about privacy and the Internet.

Privacy Rights Clearinghouse
3108 Fifth Ave., Suite A
San Diego, CA 92103
phone: (619) 298-3396 • fax: (619) 298-5681
website: www.privacyrights.org

The Privacy Rights Clearinghouse raises consumers' awareness of how technology affects personal privacy. Its website contains information and fact sheets about online privacy, as well as privacy-related speeches, court testimony, and stories of consumers' experiences.

WiredSafety
website: www.wiredsafety.org

WiredSafety is a nonprofit group that works to educate people about online safety. Its website provides information about numerous safety issues, including cyberbullying and privacy.

For Further Research

Books

Terence Craig and Mary E. Ludloff, *Privacy and Big Data*. Sebastopol, CA: O'Reilly, 2011.

Stephen Currie, *How Is the Internet Eroding Privacy Rights?* San Diego, CA: ReferencePoint, 2014.

Kord Davis, *Ethics of Big Data: Balancing Risk and Innovation*. Sebastopol, CA: O'Reilly, 2012.

Newton Lee, *Facebook Nation: Total Information Awareness*. New York: Springer, 2013.

Robert H. Sloan and Richard Warner, *Unauthorized Access: The Crisis in Online Privacy and Security*. Boca Raton, FL: CRC, 2013.

Daniel J. Solove, *Nothing to Hide: The False Tradeoff Between Privacy and Security*. New Haven, CT: Yale University Press, 2011.

Steve Weisman, *Fifty Ways to Protect Your Identity in a Digital Age*. Upper Saddle River, NJ: FT, 2013.

Periodicals

Charles Duhigg, "How Companies Learn Your Secrets," *New York Times*, February 16, 2012.

Jim Harper, "Get Over Your 'Privacy' Concerns," *New York Times*, December 12, 2012.

Jaron Lanier, "How Should We Think About Privacy?," *Scientific American*, November 2013.

Alice E. Marwick, "How Your Data Are Being Deeply Mined," *New York Review of Books*, January 9, 2014.

Internet Sources

Sarah Kessler, "Think You Can Live Offline Without Being Tracked? Here's What It Takes," *Fast Company*, October 15, 2013. www.fastcompany.com/3019847/think-you-can-live-offline-without-being-tracked-heres-what-it-takes.

Dennis Kügler, "The Online Privacy Debate: Understanding the Basics," IVPN, May 17, 2013. www.ivpn.net/blog/the-online-privacy-debate-understanding-the-basics.

Devin Leonard and John Tozzi, "Why Don't More Hospitals Use Electronic Health Records?," *Bloomberg Businessweek*, June 21, 2012. www.businessweek.com/articles/2012-06-21/why-dont-more-hospitals-use-electronic-health-records.

Jose Pagliery, "Online Privacy Is Dead," CNN Money, October 17, 2013. http://money.cnn.com/2013/10/17/technology/online-privacy.

Joe Pappalardo, "NSA Data Mining: How It Works," *Popular Mechanics*, September 11, 2013. www.popularmechanics.com/technology/military/news/nsa-data-mining-how-it-works-15910146.

Daniel J. Solove, "Why Privacy Matters Even If You Have 'Nothing to Hide,'" *Chronicle of Higher Education*, May 15, 2011. http://chronicle.com/article/Why-Privacy-Matters-Even-if/127461.

Cindy Waxer, "Big Data Blues: The Dangers of Data Mining," *Computerworld*, November 4, 2013. www.computerworld.com/s/article/9243719/Big_data_blues_The_dangers_of_data_mining?taxonomyId=18&pageNumber=1.

Index

About the Author

Christine Wilcox writes fiction and nonfiction for young adults and adults. She has worked as an editor, an instructional designer, and a writing instructor. She lives in Richmond, Virginia, with her husband, David, and her son, Doug.